Classification

Holly Wallace

H www.heinemann.co.uk
Visit our website to find out more information about Heinemann Library books.

To order:
☎ Phone 44 (0) 1865 888066
📄 Send a fax to 44 (0) 1865 314091
💻 Visit the Heinemann Bookshop at www.heinemann.co.uk to browse our catalogue and order online.

First published in Great Britain by Heinemann Library,
Halley Court, Jordan Hill, Oxford OX2 8EJ
a division of Reed Educational and Professional Publishing Ltd.
Heinemann is a registered trademark of Reed Educational & Professional Publishing Ltd.

OXFORD MELBOURNE AUCKLAND
JOHANNESBURG BLANTYRE GABORONE
IBADAN PORTSMOUTH (NH) USA CHICAGO

© Reed Educational and Professional Publishing Ltd 2000
The moral right of the proprietor has been asserted.

Designed by Celia Floyd
Originated by Dot Gradations
Printed by Wing King Tong, in Hong Kong

ISBN 0 431 10882 X
04 03 02 01 00
10 9 8 7 6 5 4 3 2 1

British Library Cataloguing in Publication Data

Wallace, Holly
  Classification. – (Life processes)
  1. Biology – Juvenile literature 2. Natural history – Classification – Juvenile literature
  I. Title
  578'.012

Acknowledgements

The Publishers would like to thank the following for permission to reproduce photographs:

Bruce Coleman: Hans Reinhard pg.24; *Mary Evans Picture Library*: pg.4; NHPA: Martin Harvey p.5, pg.29, Laurie Campbell pg.6, pg.9, MI Walker pg.6, Andy Rouse pg.7, ANT pg.8, pg.23, Stephen Dalton pg.8, pg.16, pg.20, pg. 28, Alberto Nardi pg.10, EA Janes pg.11, Daniel Zupanc pg.12, Anthony Bannister pg.13, pg.15, pg.28, NA Callow pg.14, GI Bernard pg.16, John Shaw pg.17, Norbert Wu pg.18, Daniel Heuclin pg.19, pg.22, pg.25, LUTRA pg.21, Christophe Ratier pg.25, Nigel J Dennis pg.27; *Photodisc*: pg.7, pg.26.

Cover photograph reproduced with permission of NHPA.

Every effort has been made to contact copyright holders of any material reproduced in this book. Any omissions will be rectified in subsequent printings if notice is given to the Publisher.

Any words appearing in the text in bold, **like this**, are explained in the glossary.

Contents

Introduction

The six books in this series explore the features and life processes that keep animals and plants alive. *Classification* looks at how scientists have developed a special system for identifying and naming living things so that a particular organism can be recognized all over the world. It also explains why living things are split into groups, according to their main characteristics, and describes key examples from the major classification groups.

What is classification?

There are amazing numbers of living things on Earth. Scientists use the word '**organism**' to describe anything that is alive. But they also need a way of identifying individual **species** from among the millions that exist. To do this, they divide living things into groups. This is called classification, or **taxonomy**. It is similar to the system used in a library where each book is given a code or number to make it easier to find.

Linnaeus's system

The modern system of classification was devised by the Swedish scientist, Carl von Linné (1707–1778). He gave each known living thing a two-part **Latin** name. For example, a tiger is *Panthera tigris*. The two parts work like your surname and first name, showing which family the organism belongs to and identifying it as an individual. Latin was used so that the name was the same all over the world and could be understood by everyone. Von Linné even Latinized his own name to Carolus Linnaeus. Today, we use Latin and Latin-like names. For example, the name of the scientist who discovered a new species is often Latinized and used as part of the name of the species.

Carl von Linné.

Common and scientific names

Many living things have a common name as well as a scientific (Latin) name. But the same common name might refer to several different animals. For example, you find badgers in Europe and in the USA. But they are not the same animal. Using their scientific names, *Meles meles* (European badger) and *Taxidea taxus* (American badger), avoids any confusion.

How does classification work?

Scientists divide living things into groups, depending on the features that they have in common. You can see the main groups below.

- Kingdoms – These are the largest groups. They include the animal kingdom and the plant kingdom.
- Phyla (singular: phylum) – Similar classes of living things are grouped into phyla.
- Classes – Similar orders are grouped into classes.
- Orders – Similar families are grouped into orders.
- Families – Related genera are grouped into families.
- Genera (singular: genus) – Similar species are grouped into genera. They all have similar features.
- Species – These are the smallest groups. Members of a species can breed together to produce young.

Tiger classification table

This table shows how classification works for one species, the tiger (*Panthera tigris*).

Kingdom:	*Animalia* (animals)
Phylum:	*Chordata* (**chordates**)
Sub-phylum:	*Vertebrata* (**vertebrates** – have backbones)
Class:	*Mammalia* (mammals)
Order:	*Carnivora* (carnivores – eat only meat)
Family:	*Felidae* (cats)
Genus:	*Panthera*
Species:	*tigris*

Tiger (***Panthera tigris***).

Did you know?

Scientists have no real idea how many species of living things exist on Earth. About two million have been described and classified but the actual number may be ten times higher. New species of plants and animals are being discovered each year.

Five kingdoms

The largest group of classification is the kingdom. At one time, scientists only recognized two kingdoms of living things, the plant kingdom and the animal kingdom. But many **organisms** do not fit into these two groups. They are neither plants nor animals, or they have features of both. Today, we divide living things into five kingdoms.

Moneran kingdom

Monerans are tiny, single-celled organisms such as bacteria and blue-green **algae**. They are thought to be one of the most ancient forms of life on Earth. Their cells are very simple and, unlike all other living things, do not have a **nucleus**. Over 3000 **species** of monerans are known.

Protist kingdom

The protist kingdom is made up mostly of organisms that have a single cell with a nucleus. For example, an amoeba is a protist. There are more than 28,000 known species of protists. All protists live in damp places or in water.

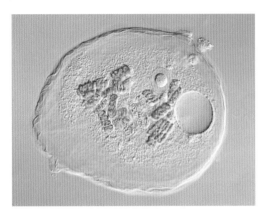

An amoeba is a protist.

Fungi kingdom

Fungi are organisms such as moulds, mushrooms and mildew. The body of a fungus is made up of a network of threads called hyphae. Unlike plant cells, hyphae cells do not contain **chlorophyll** and so cannot make their own food by **photosynthesis**. Instead, fungi feed by absorbing food from other organisms, both alive and dead. There are about 75,000 known fungi species.

Fly agaric (*Amanita muscaria*), a highly poisonous fungus.

Plant kingdom

Plant cells have rigid cell walls made of **cellulose**. Their cells contain a green substance called chlorophyll, which they use to make their own food by photosynthesis. For this they need water and sunlight. Plants do not move from place to place. There are more than 400,000 known plant species.

Animal kingdom

Animals are made up of many cells that form specialized **tissues**, **organs** and **organ systems**. Animal cells do not have rigid walls, and they cannot make their own food. Most animals have to move around to find food and escape from danger. There are about 1,500,000 known species of animals.

Using a key

You can work out the identity of an organism by using a key, like the very simple one below for big cats. A key is a set of questions and each answer leads to another question. This continues until you find the name of the organism.

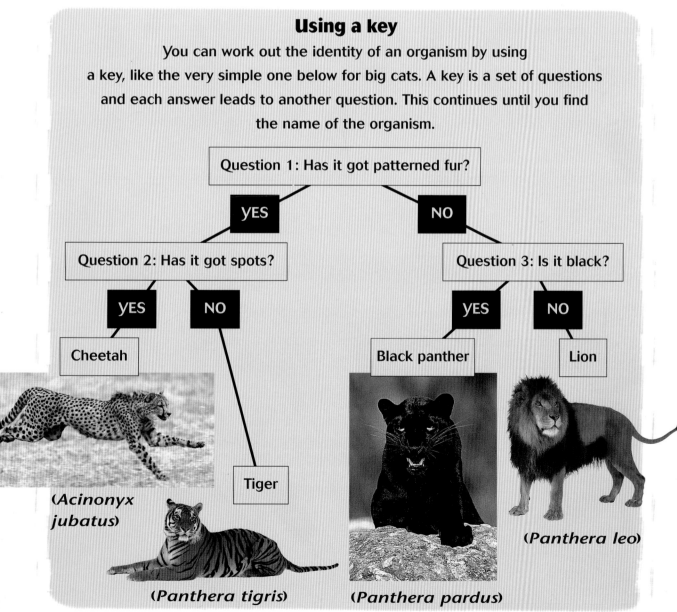

Question 1: Has it got patterned fur?

YES — Question 2: Has it got spots?
NO — Question 3: Is it black?

Question 2: YES — Cheetah / NO — Tiger

Question 3: YES — Black panther / NO — Lion

Cheetah *(Acinonyx jubatus)*

Tiger *(Panthera tigris)*

Black panther *(Panthera pardus)*

Lion *(Panthera leo)*

Plants without flowers

The plant kingdom is divided into flowering plants and plants that do not produce flowers. Plants without flowers have been growing on Earth for some 300 million years. The prehistoric ancestors of modern horsetails and clubmosses grew up to 30 metres tall, higher than a house. Most non-flowering plants grow from tiny, dust-like specks called **spores**. The spores are made and released in their thousands, then carried away by the wind. If they land in a suitable place, they grow into new plants.

Giant bull kelp seaweed (*Durvillea antarctica*).

Algae

Algae are very simple, non-flowering plants, with no proper roots, leaves or stems. They usually grow in water and range in size from microscopic, single-celled plants to gigantic seaweeds. They are classified according to their colour, red, green or brown. Plants give off oxygen as waste when they **photosynthesise**. Sea-**algae** produce about 80 per cent of all the oxygen in the air. Some biologists classify all types of algae as protists (see page 6).

Mosses and liverworts

Mosses and liverworts are mainly small, ground-hugging plants that live in damp places. They do not have flowers but produce their spores in a small capsule that is held up on a tiny stalk. When the capsule opens, the spores are carried away on the wind.

A spore capsule of a star moss (*Polytrichum* species) ready to release the spores into the air.

Ferns, horsetails and clubmosses

Ferns, horsetails and clubmosses also grow from spores. Ferns are plants with frond-like leaves that grow from underground stems. Some have rusty spots under their leaves. These are spore-bearing structures called sporangia.

A monkey puzzle tree (*Araucaria araucana*).

Conifers

Conifers (class *Gymnospermae*) are trees such as pines, larches and redwoods. Unlike the other non-flowering plants, they grow new plants from seeds, formed when male **pollen** joins with female **ovules**. But they do not produce flowers. Instead, their pollen, ovules and seeds grow in woody cones. There are about 550 **species** of conifers.

Did you know?

Lichens are a cross between a fungus and an alga. The alga provides the fungus with food made by photosynthesis. In turn, the fungus protects the alga and provides it with water. It is a highly successful combination. Lichens are extremely hardy and can survive in very cold or hostile conditions.

Simple Plants		Ferns and Horsetails		Conifers	
Kingdom:	*Plantae* (plants)	Kingdom:	*Plantae* (plants)	Kingdom:	*Plantae* (plants)
Phylum:	*Byrophyta* (plants with simple roots, stems and leaves but no **vascular tissue**)	Phyla:	*Filicinophyta* (ferns); *Sphenophyta* (horsetails); *Lycophyta* (clubmosses)	Phyla:	*Coniferophyta* (conifers); *Cycadophyta* (cycads); *Ginkophyta* (ginkgoes); *Gnetophyta* (gnetophytes - tropical and desert shrubs)
Classes:	*Hepaticae* (liverworts); *Musci* (mosses); *Anthocerotae* (hornworts)				

Flowering plants

Flowering plants belong to the class *Angiospermae*. Flowers contain the plants' male and female parts, which are needed to make seeds that will grow into new plants. Some flowers have both male and female parts in the same flower, others are either male or female. The male parts make a fine powder called **pollen**. For a seed to grow, the pollen must join with a female **ovule**. This is called **pollination**. Pollen is often carried from flower to flower by the wind or by animals. Flowering plants are by far the biggest group of plants with about 250,000 **species**. They first grew on Earth about a hundred million years ago.

Monocotyledons

Flowering plants can be divided into two sub-classes, monocotyledons and dicotyledons. A cotyledon is a tiny leaf inside a seed. Until the new plant grows its first leaves, it lives off food stored in the cotyledon. Monocotyledons have only one of these leaves in their seeds. Other features include narrow leaves with parallel **veins** and usually three parts to their flowers. Irises, daffodils and grasses are monocotyledons.

A field of poppies (*Papaver* species) – poppies are dicotyledons.

Dicotyledons

Dicotyledons have two cotyledons in their seeds. They include plants such as daisies, carrots, cabbages, oak trees, cacti and roses. Most have broad leaves with a branching pattern of veins. Their flowers are usually divided into four or five parts.

Trees

Trees are plants with tall, woody trunks instead of stems. The two most common groups of trees are conifers (see page 9) and broadleaved trees. Conifers make seeds but do not make flowers. Broadleaved trees are flowering plants. For example, cherry trees belong to the rose family. Most broadleaved trees are **deciduous**. This means that they lose their leaves once a year..

A beech tree (*Fagus sylvatica*) in autumn — beeches are deciduous.

Flowering plant classification	
Kingdom:	*Plantae* (plants)
Phylum:	*Angiospermophyta* (angiosperms, or plants with flowers and fruits)
Classes:	*Monocotyledonae* (monocotyledons, eg: daffodils, grasses) *Dicotyledonae* (dicotyledons, eg: oak trees, roses)
Number of species:	more than 250,000

Invertebrates

Invertebrates are animals that do not have **vertebrae** (backbones) or skeletons inside their bodies. With some 950,000 species, there are far more invertebrates than **vertebrates** on Earth. About 97 per cent of animal **species** are invertebrates. They are divided into many different groups, including insects (see page 14), molluscs, worms, starfish and jellyfish.

An edible snail (*Helix pomatia*).

Molluscs

After insects, molluscs make up the second largest group of invertebrates. All molluscs have a soft body that is often protected by a hard shell. Most live in water. Molluscs include snails and slugs (class *Gastropoda*); clams and mussels (class *Bivalvia*); and octopuses and squid (class *Cephalopoda*). Bivalves have two parts to their shells. Cephalopods have a small shell hidden inside their bodies.

Jellyfish and sea-anemones

Jellyfish, sea-anenomes and corals belong to a group of invertebrates called cnidarians (phylum *Cnidaria*). They have soft, circular bodies and mouths surrounded by stinging tentacles used for catching **prey**. All jellyfish can sting, but the box jellyfish (*Chironex fleckeri*) of Australia is deadly. Its poison can kill a person within four minutes of being stung.

Worms

Worms, such as earthworms, leeches and lugworms, are annelids (phylum *Annelida*). They have long, tubular bodies divided into segments. The longest earthworm is the giant *Michrochaetus rappi* from South Africa, which grows over a metre long. Earthworms spend most of their lives underground. Their burrows help to keep the soil healthy by allowing air and water to circulate.

'Spiny-skinned'

Starfish, sea-urchins and their relatives are echinoderms (phylum *Echinodermata*). Their name means 'spiny-skinned'. Echinoderms have chalky skeletons and bodies arranged in five parts. Many starfish, for example, have five arms. If a starfish loses an arm, it can grow another one. Underneath each arm are rows of '**tube feet**' that the starfish uses to move and grip its prey.

Two echinoderms — a starfish and a sea-urchin.

Invertebrate classification

Kingdom:	*Animalia* (animals)
Major phyla:	1 *Cnidaria* (coelenterates)
	2 *Ctenophora* (comb jellies)
	3 *Platyhelminthes* (flatworms)
	4 *Nematoda* (roundworms)
	5 *Mollusca* (molluscs)
	6 *Annelida* (segmented worms)
	7 *Arthropoda* (arthropods)

Mollusc classification

Kingdom:	*Animalia* (animals)
Phylum:	*Mollusca* (molluscs)
Classes:	1 *Polyplacophora* (chitons)
	2 *Gastropoda* (snails, slugs)
	3 *Bivalvia* (clams, mussels)
	4 *Cephalopoda* (squid, octopuses)
	(plus 3 minor classes)
Number of orders:	about 45
Number of species:	about 75,000

Arthropods

The biggest group of **invertebrates** is the arthropods (phylum *Arthropoda*). It includes insects, arachnids (see pages 16–17), crustaceans, centipedes and millipedes. With over a million known **species**, it is the largest group of animals on Earth. All arthropods have bodies divided into segments and legs that bend at joints. Their soft bodies are covered with hard cases or shells called **exoskeletons**. Most arthropods have **antennae**.

Insect identification

Insects (class *Insecta*) live all over the world in all types of climate and condition. All insects have three parts to their bodies – the head, **thorax** and **abdomen**. They have six pairs of legs attached to their thorax. Most insects have two pairs of wings and can fly. Flies have only one pair of wings. Adult ants and aphids have none. Insects have **compound eyes** made up of hundreds of tiny lenses and one pair of antennae for smelling, tasting, touching and sensing vibrations in the air.

Insect classification

Kingdom:	*Animalia* (animals)
Phylum:	*Arthropoda* (arthropods)
Sub-phylum:	*Uniramia* (one pair of antennae)
Class:	*Insecta* (insects)
Number of orders:	19
Number of species:	about 1 million

Honeybees (*Apis mellifera*) are typical insects.

Crustaceans

Like insects, crustaceans (sub-phylum *Crustacea*) are arthropods. Most of the 44,000 species of crustaceans live in the sea. Woodlice (class *Isopoda*) are unusual because they live on land. Crustaceans have bodies divided into many segments, each with a pair of jointed legs for walking and swimming. They have two pairs of antennae, and most are covered in hard shells. Crustaceans include crabs, lobsters, barnacles, water fleas, shrimps and woodlice.

Centipedes and millipedes

Centipedes (class *Chilopoda*) and millipedes (class *Diplopoda*) are myriapods, or 'many-legged' arthropods. Both have long, many-segmented bodies and, from a distance, look quite alike. But centipedes have one pair of legs on each body segment while millipedes have two. Millipedes are plant-eaters, while centipedes are fierce **predators**, paralysing their **prey** with poison fangs. There are about 11,000 species of centipedes and millipedes.

A spirobolid millepede (family *Spirobolidae*).

Did you know?

There are more different kinds of insects than all other species of animal put together. According to some experts, nearly 90 per cent of all animals are insects. At least one million species have already been described and scientists are finding new species all the time, at the rate of about 8–10,000 species a year. There may be another 30 million species waiting to be found!

Arachnids

Spiders and their relatives, the scorpions, ticks and mites, make up the class of animals called arachnids. Like insects, arachnids are **invertebrates**. Arachnids are also arthropods. There are important differences between insects and arachnids. Arachnids have only two parts to their bodies – the **cephalothorax** (the head and thorax joined together), and a large **abdomen**. They have four pairs of legs and do not have wings or **antennae**.

Spider spinners

Spiders (order *Araneae*) are famous for their silk-making skills. The silk is made inside the spider's body and squeezed out through tiny nozzles, called spinnerets, at its rear. Some spiders weave silk webs to catch their **prey**. Others are hunters, chasing their prey on the ground. Once the prey is caught, the spider bites and kills it with its poison fangs. There are about 35,000 known **species** of spiders with perhaps as many as 200,000 still waiting to be discovered.

A huge tropical spider devouring a tree frog.

A yellow desert scorpion (*Butuus quinquestriatus*).

Sting in the tail

Scorpions (order *Scorpionida*) have a very distinctive appearance. Like spiders, they have four pairs of legs, and they also have a pair of strong, pincer-like claws, used for grabbing prey. Many scorpions have venomous stings in their tails that they mainly use in self-defence. There are about 800 known species of scorpions.

Ticks and mites

Ticks and mites (order *Acari*) are **parasites**, living on other animals and plants, and feeding on their sap, blood, fur and feathers. Some common mites live on household dust that is mostly made up of flakes of dead human skin! Most are tiny, often less than one millimetre long. But they can be deadly, spreading diseases in humans, animals and food crops. There are about 30,000 known species of ticks and mites.

A wood tick (*Dermacentor andersoni*).

Arachnid classification	
Kingdom:	*Animalia* (animals)
Phylum:	*Arthropoda* (arthropods)
Sub-phylum:	*Chelicerata* (chelicerates – animals with pincer-like mouthparts)
Class:	*Arachnida* (arachnids)
Number of orders:	11
Number of species:	about 75,000

Fish

Fish are **vertebrates**. There are as many **species** of fish as all other vertebrates (amphibians, reptiles, birds and mammals) put together. Fish are **cold-blooded**. They live in water, both fresh and salty, and 'breathe' in oxygen through **gills**. Fish are designed for swimming with muscular, streamlined bodies often covered in scales, and with fins instead of limbs. Fish were the earliest known vertebrates on Earth. The first fish appeared some 515 million years ago.

Rubbery skeletons

Sharks, rays and skates belong to the group of **cartilaginous** fish (class *Chondrichthyes*). Instead of bone, they have skeletons made of rubbery, flexible **cartilage**. They also have a series of separate gill slits along each side of the body. With its razor-sharp teeth and man-eating reputation, the most famous shark is the great white. But the largest shark is the enormous whale shark that feeds on **plankton**, filtered from the water. This giant can grow up to eighteen metres long, but it is harmless.

Carribbean reef sharks (*Carcharhinus perezi*) are cartilaginous fish.

Bony fish

More than 95 per cent of all fish are bony fish (class *Osteichthyes*). As their name suggests, bony fish have skeletons made of bone. Their gills are covered by a flap with a single opening at the rear. This group includes fish such as herrings, salmon, angler fish, eels and carp. It is found all over the world, from vast oceans to tiny ponds. The longest bony fish is the striking-looking oarfish. It can grow over nine metres long and looks like a silvery ribbon, with a long, red fin along its back.

How fish breathe

Fish use their gills to breathe oxygen dissolved in the water. A fish swims along, opening and closing its mouth. As it opens its mouth, it gulps in water. As it closes its mouth, it pushes the water out again through its gills. As the water passes over the gills, the fish's blood vessels absorb oxygen from the water and release waste carbon dioxide into the water to be pumped out.

Did you know?

Despite its strange, S-shaped body, the seahorse is a true fish. It belongs to the same group as sticklebacks and pipefish (order *Gasterosteiformes*). Seahorses are weak, slow swimmers, using their delicate back fins to help them move along. More often they are seen clinging to seaweed with their sensitive tails.

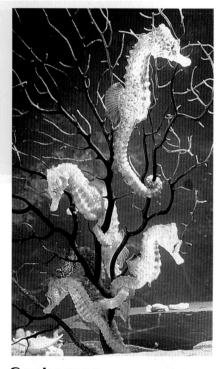

Seahorses (*Hippocampus hippocampus*) are really fish.

Fish classification

Kingdom:	*Animalia* (animals)
Phylum:	*Chordata* (**chordates**)
Sub-phylum:	*Vertebrata* (vertebrates)
Classes:	1 Lampreys and hagfish (jawless fish)
	2 *Chondrichthyes* (fish with skeletons made of cartilage)
	3 *Osteichthyes* (fish with skeletons made of bone)
Number of orders:	20
Number of species:	about 24,000 (with about 100 new species discovered every year)

Amphibians

The ancestors of modern amphibians were the first **vertebrates** to leave the water to search for food and to live on land. They first appeared on Earth about 370 million years ago. Amphibians are **cold-blooded** vertebrates. They have smooth, scaleless skin. Their young breathe through **gills**, like fish. Adult amphibians have lungs, but they also breathe through their skins, which they must keep moist to absorb oxygen properly.

Frogs and toads

Frogs and toads belong to the order *Anura*. They look very similar but there are several ways of telling them apart. Frogs have smoother skin and longer legs, for jumping. Toads may have lumpy warts on their skins and squatter bodies. Most frogs and toads live on or near the ground, and feed on fast-moving **prey** such as insects and spiders. There are about 3800 known **species** of frogs and toads, or anurans, living all over the world. About 20 new species are discovered each year.

A common frog (order *Anura*).

The name amphibian comes from a Greek word *amphibios*, which means 'a being with a double life'. This describes how amphibians can live both in water and on land. Most amphibians spend their adult lives on land. But they must return to the water to breed and lay their eggs.

Newts and salamanders

Newts and salamanders belong to the order *Urodela* or *Caudata*. They live in the damp undergrowth near water and feed on **invertebrates** such as slugs, snails and worms. They have longer bodies and shorter legs than anurans, and long, distinctive tails. When a newt or salamander loses a leg or part of its tail, it can grow a new one. There are about 360 known species of newts and salamanders.

A fire salamander
(*Salamandra salamandra*).

Caecilians

Caecilians belong to the third order of amphibians, *Gymnophiona*. Their long, cylindrical shape makes them look more like small snakes than amphibians. Caecilians do not have legs and are nearly blind. They live in water or burrow in soft earth, feeding on earthworms and other invertebrates. There are about 170 known species of caecilians, living in the tropics. Most are about 50 centimetres long, but some reach lengths of 1.5 metres.

Amphibian classification	
Kingdom:	*Animalia* (animals)
Phylum:	*Chordata* (**chordates**)
Sub-phylum:	*Vertebrata* (vertebrates)
Class:	*Amphibia* (amphibians)
Number of orders:	3
Number of species:	about 4500

Reptiles

Snakes, lizards, crocodiles and turtles are all types of reptile. Reptiles are **vertebrates**. Because they are **cold-blooded**, they usually live in warm places where the Sun heats their bodies up and makes them active. Reptiles are much better adapted for life on land than amphibians. Their scaly skin protects their bodies and stops them drying out, and they lay eggs protected by tough, leathery shells. Some reptiles give birth to live young. There are about 6500 known **species** of reptiles, divided into four main orders.

Snakes and lizards

With about 6000 species, snakes and lizards (order *Squamata*) form the largest group of reptiles. Although snakes look quite different from lizards, scientists believe that they evolved from lizard-like ancestors that had two pairs of legs. Lizards range in size from tiny geckos (family *Gekkonidae*) to the huge Komodo dragon (*Varanus komodoensis*) of Indonesia. The longest snake in the world is the reticulated python (*Python reticulatus*) of South-east Asia, which can grow up to ten metres long.

A red spitting cobra (*Naja pallida*) coiled around her eggs.

Alligators and crocodiles

Alligators and crocodiles (order *Crocodilia*) are the largest living reptiles. These giants are covered in large, hard scales, strengthened with bone, to form 'armour plating'. They are well adapted for life in water, using their powerful tails for swimming. Their eyes and nostrils are on top of their heads so that they can lie submerged but still see and breathe. Crocodilians are fierce **predators**. They drag **prey** under water and tear it apart with their sharp, pointed teeth.

Turtles and tortoises

Turtles, tortoises and terrapins make up the order *Chelonia*. They have bony shells for protection and beak-like jaws instead of teeth. They live in oceans, rivers and on land, and feed on plants and small animals. Some turtles and tortoises can live for a very long time. The record for any land animal is 152 years for a Marion's tortoise (*Geochelone gigantea*).

Reptile classification	
Kingdom:	*Animalia* (animals)
Phylum:	*Chordata* (**chordates**)
Sub-phylum:	*Vertebrata* (vertebrates)
Class:	*Reptilia* (reptiles)
Number of orders:	4 (major)
Number of species:	about 6500

Did you know?

The tuatara (*Sphenodon punctatus*) is the only living member of an ancient order of reptiles (order *Rhynchocephalia*). Its ancestors appeared about 220 million years ago, before the first dinosaurs. Today, tuatara are only found in New Zealand. Their name comes from a local Maori word meaning 'peaks on the back', which refers to the spiky crest growing along the tuatara's back and tail.

A tuatara (*Sphenodon punctatus*).

Birds

Birds are **warm-blooded vertebrates**. They are the only animals whose bodies are covered with feathers. Most birds can fly. Birds breathe air through lungs. They have beaks but no teeth and produce their young by laying eggs with hard shells. Birds are found all over the world, in city centres, steamy rainforests and at the icy poles. They range in size from the huge African ostrich (*Struthio camelus*), which stands two metres tall, to tiny bee hummingbirds (*Mellisuga helenae*) from Central America, which are no bigger than butterflies.

Perching birds

The largest order of birds is the perching birds (order *Passeriformes*). It includes over 5500 **species**, almost 60 per cent of all known birds. Passerines have four toes on their feet, three pointing forwards and one pointing backwards, for gripping on to branches.

The painted bunting (*Passerina ciris*) is a perching bird.

Bird classification

Kingdom:	*Animalia* (animals)
Phylum:	*Chordata* (**chordates**)
Sub-phylum:	*Vertebrata* (vertebrates)
Class:	*Aves* (birds)
Number of orders:	23
Number of species:	more than 8500

Did you know?

The first bird lived on Earth about 150 million years ago. It was given the **Latin** name *Archaeopteryx* which means 'ancient wings'. Fossils found in the 1860s show that it was about the size of a pigeon, with feathers, wings and a wishbone in its skeleton, like a modern bird. But it also had teeth and a long, bony tail, like a reptile. From creatures like *Archaeopteryx*, scientists have been able to show that birds are the living descendants of dinosaurs.

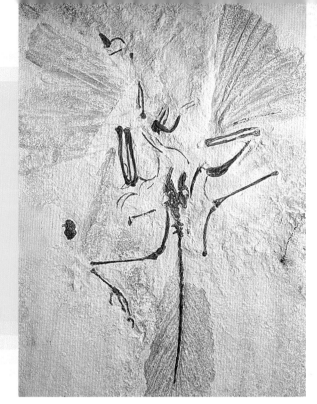

An *Archaeopteryx* fossil found in Germany.

Flightless birds

Some birds, such as ostriches and penguins, have wings but cannot fly. Ostriches (order *Struthioniformes*) are the largest birds in the world. They are too heavy to fly but can run at more than 70 kilometres an hour, faster than a racehorse. Penguins (order *Sphenisciformes*) look clumsy on land but seem to 'fly' under water. Using its wings as flippers, the gentoo penguin (*Pygoscelis papua*) can reach speeds of about 40 kilometres an hour, three times faster than the fastest human swimmer.

The ostrich (*Struthio camelus*) is a flightless bird.

Mammals

There are more than 4000 **species** of mammals, ranging from huge elephants and whales to tiny bats and shrews. It is the class to which human beings also belong. Mammals are **warm-blooded vertebrates** that breathe air using lungs. They all suckle their young on milk and are the only animals that produce milk. They also look after their young until they are old enough to fend for themselves. Mammals are the only animals with earflaps to channel sound down into their ears.

Marsupials

Marsupials (order *Marsupiala*) are mammals with pouches. They include kangaroos, koalas and wombats. Their new-born young are very tiny and weak. After birth, they crawl into their mother's pouch where they feed on milk and grow.

Kangaroos are marsupials.

Monotremes

Three species of mammal, the duck-billed platypus, the long-beaked echidna and the short-beaked echidna, belong to the order *Monotremata*. Monotremes are mammals that lay eggs. A female duck-billed platypus (*Ornithorhynchus anatinus*) lays her soft, sticky eggs in a riverbank tunnel. When the young hatch, she feeds them on milk like other mammals.

Mammal classification	
Kingdom:	*Animalia* (animals)
Phylum:	*Chordata* (**chordates**)
Sub-phylum:	*Vertebrata* (vertebrates)
Class:	*Mammalia* (mammals)
Sub-classes:	1 *Prototheria* (egg-laying)
	2 *Theria* (do not lay eggs)
Infra-classes:	1 *Eutheria* (**placental**)
	2 *Metatheria* (non-placental)
Number of orders:	19
Number of species:	more than 4000

Mammal orders

Order	Examples	No of Species
Artiodacytyla	Camels, pigs, cattle	c 180
Carnivora	Cats, bears, dogs	c 250
Cetacea	Whales, dolphins	72
Chiroptera	Bats	c 800
Dermoptera	Flying lemurs	2
Edentata	Anteaters, sloths	29
Hyracoidea	Hyraxes	c 6
Insectivora	Moles, shrews	c 350
Lagomorpha	Rabbits, hares	c 60
Monotremata	Platypus, spiny anteater	3
Marsupiala	Kangaroos, koalas	c 275
Perissodactyla	Tapirs, rhinos, horses	15
Pholidota	Pangolins	7
Pinnipedia	Seals, sealions, walrus	34
Primates	Lemurs, monkeys, humans	c 200
Proboscidea	Elephants	2
Rodentia	Mice, porcupines, beavers	c 1750
Sirenia	Dugongs, manatees	4
Tubulidentata	Aardvark	1

Did you know?

The aardvark (*Orycteropus afer*) is the only living member of its order (*Tubulidendata*). This unusual ant-eating mammal lives in the **grasslands** of Africa. Its body is specialized for burrowing after its food, with long, spade-shaped claws and powerful back legs. Instead of running away from enemies, it digs a hole and hides. As it digs, it folds back its ears and closes its nostrils to keep out the soil.

An aardvark (*Orycteropus afer*).

More mammals

Most mammals are **placental** mammals. Their babies grow inside their mothers' bodies until they are fully formed. They receive nourishment from their mother through her placenta, and when they are born, they look like smaller versions of their parents. Placental mammals include whales, bats and human beings.

Flying mammals

Bats (order *Chiroptera*) make up nearly a quarter of all mammal **species**. Bats are the only mammals that can truly fly, although some mammals can glide. The name *Chiroptera* is **Latin** for 'hand-wings'. This is

Geoffroy's long-nosed bat (*Anoura geoffroyi*).

because a bat's wings have evolved from its hands and arms. Its finger bones are very long, with leathery skin stretched between them, leaving the thumb free. The wings are also attached to the bat's back legs and tail. There are two main groups of bat — large fruit bats, or flying foxes, and smaller insect-eaters.

Did you know?

The African elephant (*Loxodonta africana*) is the world's largest living land mammal. An adult bull (male) elephant can weigh more than 5 tonnes and stand 3 metres tall. Incredibly, their closest mammal relative is believed to be the rabbit-sized hyrax (order *Hyracoidea*). They are thought to have originated from the same mammal group some 55 million years ago.

Cape hyraxes (*Procavia capensis*).

Sea mammals

There are about 120 species of sea mammals, belonging to three orders – *Cetacea* (whales and dolphins), *Pinnipedia* (seals, sealions and walruses) and *Sirenia* (dugongs and manatees). They include the gigantic blue whale, the largest mammal that has ever lived. Blue whales (*Balaenoptera musculus*) can weigh 130 tonnes and grow more than 30 metres long.

Human mammals

Human beings (*Homo sapiens*) belong to the order of primates. There are about 200 species of primates, divided into two groups. The anthropoids include apes (chimpanzees, gorillas, orang-utans and gibbons), monkeys and humans. The prosimians include bush-babies and lemurs. Humans are very closely related to apes. Gorillas and chimpanzees are more closely related to us than they are to orang-utans.

Young chimpanzees (*Pan troglodytes*).

Human classification	
Kingdom:	*Animalia* (animals)
Phylum:	*Chordata* (**chordates**)
Sub-phylum:	*Vertebrata* (**vertebrates**)
Class:	*Mammalia* (mammals)
Sub-class:	*Eutheria* (placental)
Order:	*Primates* (primates)
Family:	*Hominidae* (homonids)
Species:	*Homo sapiens* (humans)

Conclusion

Think how difficult it would be to find the book you wanted in a bookshop or library if the books were jumbled up together. Organizing them according to subject matter, author or title makes them much easier to find. This is why classification is so useful for identifying living things. Once you know the scientific name of a plant or animal, you can find out what it is and exactly where in the living world it belongs.

Glossary

abdomen   the end part of an insect's or arachnid's body

algae   very simple plants found in salt and fresh water

antennae   feeler-like sense organs on an insect's head. They are used for touching, sensing changes in temperature and detecting tastes and smells.

cartilage   a rubbery, flexible tissue which makes up the skeletons of such fish such as sharks, instead of bone

cartilaginous   this means to be made of cartilage

cellulose   a tough material which makes the fibres found in plant cell walls

cephalothorax   the front part of an arachnid's body, made up of the head and thorax joined together

chlorophyll   a green pigment (colouring) found inside plant cells. It absorbs energy from sunlight for use in photosynthesis.

chordates   organisms which, at some time in their lives, have a stiff, skeletal rod of cells running along and supporting their spinal cord

cold-blooded   animals, such as fish, amphibians and reptiles, which cannot control their own body temperature. They rely on the weather to warm them up or cool them down.

compound eyes   the special eyes of many insects. Each eye is made up of hundreds of tiny, individual lenses.

deciduous   trees and plants that regularly shed their leaves

exoskeletons   the tough, outer coat or shell of invertebrates such as insects or crabs. It protects and supports their soft bodies.

gills   thin, feathery organs which fish use for breathing in oxygen from the water

grasslands   large, open, flat areas covered in grasses and low bushes. Grasslands cover about a quarter of the land on Earth.

infra-classes   two special sub-classes found only in mammals

invertebrates   animals which do not have backbones or skeletons inside their bodies

Latin   a language originally spoken in Ancient Rome. Many modern languages are based on Latin. It is also the language used in science to describe living things.

nucleus   a rounded structure inside a cell. It is the cell's control centre, regulating everything that happens inside the cell.

organism   the scientific word for a living thing

organs   groups of different tissues in a living thing's body. Your heart and lungs are examples of organs.

organ systems   groups of organs working together in a living thing's body. Your digestive system is an organ system. It uses various organs, such as your stomach and intestines.

ovules   the female sex cells of a flowering plant or conifer. After fertilization, ovules become seeds.

parasites   plants or animals which live on or in other plants or animals and get all their food from them

photosynthesis   the process by which green plants make food from carbon dioxide and water, using energy from sunlight absorbed by their chlorophyll

placental   placental mammals are those whose young develop inside their mother's bodies until they are fully formed

plankton   tiny plants and animals which live in water and provide food for many other animals

pollen   tiny grains which are the male sex cells of flowering plants and conifers

pollination   the transfer of pollen from a male flower to a female flower or from the male part of a flower to the female part so that fertilization can happen

predators   animals which hunt and kill other animals for food

prey   animals that are hunted and eaten by other animals

species   a group of organisms which are grouped together because they have similar features and can breed with each other

spores   tiny, dust-like specks produced by fungi and many other non-flowering plants. They grow into new plants.

taxonomy   the way in which living things are divided into groups, based on the features they have in common. This makes them easier to identify and study. It is also called classification.

thorax   the middle part of an insect's body bearing the legs and wings

tissues   groups of cells in a living thing's body that have a special job to do. Bones and muscle are types of tissues.

tube feet   tiny, tube-like tentacles which starfish and other echinoderms use for breathing, moving and grasping food

vascular tissue   the system of tubes called xylem and phloem inside a plant which carries water and food around the plant

veins   part of a plant's vascular tissue. Veins also help to strengthen a plant's leaves and support them to give them their shape.

vertebrae   the interlinked bones in a vertebrate's backbone

vertebrates   animals with backbones and skeletons inside their bodies. Fish, amphibians, reptiles, birds and mammals are all vertebrates.

warm-blooded   animals that can control their own body temperature so that it stays the same whatever the weather outside. This allows them to be active in the heat or cold.

Index